practical NLP

**Steve Bavister and
Amanda Vickers**

For UK order enquiries: please contact Bookpoint Ltd,
130 Milton Park, Abingdon, Oxon OX14 4SB.
Telephone: +44 (0) 1235 827720. *Fax*: +44 (0) 1235 400454.
Lines are open 09.00–17.00, Monday to Saturday, with a 24-hour
message answering service. Details about our titles and how to
order are available at www.hoddereducation.com

British Library Cataloguing in Publication Data: a catalogue record for
this title is available from the British Library.

First published in UK 2011 by Hodder Education, part of Hachette UK,
338 Euston Road, London NW1 3BH.

Typeset by MPS Limited, a Macmillan Company.

Printed in Great Britain for Hodder Education, an Hachette UK Company,
338 Euston Road, London NW1 3BH, by CPI Cox & Wyman, Reading,
Berkshire RG1 8EX.

The publisher has used its best endeavours to ensure that the URLs for
external websites referred to in this book are correct and active at the time of
going to press. However, the publisher and the author have no responsibility
for the websites and can make no guarantee that a site will remain live or
that the content will remain relevant, decent or appropriate.

Hachette UK's policy is to use papers that are natural, renewable and
recyclable products and made from wood grown in sustainable forests.
The logging and manufacturing processes are expected to conform to the
environmental regulations of the country of origin.

Impression number   10 9 8 7 6 5 4 3 2 1
Year   2015 2014 2013 2012 2011

Contents

what is NLP?

Some people initially struggle to understand what Neuro-Linguistic Programming (NLP) is or grasp its essence. That's because it has both enormous breadth and depth, and can be used in so many different ways.

The most useful way of thinking of NLP is as a practical form of applied psychology – as a 'User's Manual for the Brain'. The 'neuro' part relates to neurology and the ways in which we process information we receive from our five senses. 'Linguistic' relates to the use of language systems to code, organize and attribute meanings to our internal representations of the world. 'Programming' is about the way in which our experience is coded, stored and transformed to create habits and 'programmes'.

NLP was developed in California in the 1970s by a mathematician, Richard Bandler, and a linguist, John Grinder, who drew upon a multitude of disciplines, including systems thinking, psychotherapy, cybernetics and general semantics.

Unpacking the N, the L and the P

Perhaps the easiest way of explaining NLP is to say it is a form of applied psychology. That's not the whole story, but it's how many people use it – as a means of achieving more for themselves and being more fulfilled in their personal and professional lives.

Another problem for NLP is the technical nature of the name. Happily, these days it is better known, but the reaction when you mention Neuro-Linguistic Programming from those who have never heard of it is still to ask, 'What on earth is that?' Although many of us wish the founders had come up with a name that was snappier, clearer and – for those of us who earn a living from NLP – sexier, in fact 'Neuro-Linguistic Programming' is simply an accurate description of what it is. Let's take a look at why each of the terms came to be used.

Neuro

The 'neuro' part relates to neurology, to the ways in which we process information from our five senses through our brain and nervous system.

Linguistic

'Linguistic' relates to the use of language systems – not just words but all symbol systems including gestures and postures – to code, organize and attribute meanings to our internal representations of the world, and to communicate internally and externally.

Programming

And 'programming' comes from information processing and computing science, on the premise that the way in which experience is stored, coded and transformed is similar to how software runs on a PC. By deleting, upgrading or installing our mental software, we can change how we think and, as a result, how we act.

When you link all the words up you have Neuro-Linguistic Programming, which is essentially concerned with the processes by which we create an internal representation – our experience – of the external world of 'reality' through language and our neurology.

The NLP model

We experience the world through our five senses: sight, hearing, touch, smell and taste. Because there is so much continuous information coming in our direction we consciously and unconsciously delete what we don't want to pay attention to. We filter the remaining data based on our past experiences, values and beliefs. What we end up with is incomplete and inaccurate because some of the original input has been deleted altogether and the rest has been generalized or distorted. The filtered information forms our internal map, which influences our physiology and 'state of being'. This in turn affects our behaviour.

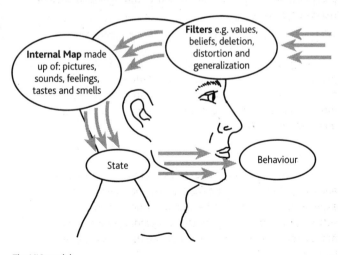

The NLP model.

The story of NLP

At the heart of NLP is the 'modelling' of human excellence – and that is where the story of NLP begins in the early 1970s, with the collaboration of Richard Bandler and John Grinder at the University of California.

Bandler, a student of mathematics with a particular interest in computer science, got involved in transcribing some audio and video seminar tapes of Fritz Perls, the father of Gestalt Therapy, and Virginia Satir, the founder of Family Therapy. He found that by copying certain aspects of their behaviour and language he could achieve similar results, and began running a Gestalt Therapy group on the campus.

John Grinder, an associate professor of linguistics at the university, was intrigued by Bandler's abilities, and reputedly said to him: 'If you teach me how to do what you do, I'll tell you what you do.'

It wasn't long before Grinder, too, could get the same kind of therapeutic results as Bandler and Perls, simply by copying what Bandler did and said. Then, by a process of subtraction – by systematically leaving various elements out – Grinder was able to determine what was essential and what was irrelevant.

Realizing they were on to something, Bandler and Grinder joined forces and went on to write the first NLP book, *The Structure of Magic*, which was published in 1975. Subtitled *A Book about Language and Therapy*, it introduced the first NLP model, the Meta Model – 12 language patterns distilled from modelling Perls and Satir.

Already the essence of NLP had been defined. By studying carefully and analysing thoroughly – modelling – those who are geniuses in their field, it's possible for anyone to copy the crucial elements and achieve the same results. If you want to be an expert golfer you need to model someone who is excellent at the game – observing what they do and say, and then asking questions about what's going on mentally. In doing so you create a template for success that anyone can use.

The crucial discovery, though, was that our subjective experience of the world has a structure, and that how we think about something affects how we experience it. Drawing on the work of Alfred Korzybski, NLP makes a clear distinction between the 'territory' – the world itself – and the internal 'map' we create of it. This is often expressed succinctly as 'The map is not the territory'.

'An attitude and a methodology'

One of the defining descriptions – 'NLP is an attitude and a methodology that leaves behind a trail of techniques' – comes from co-founder John Grinder, and is crucial to understanding NLP. So far we have talked mainly about the methodology, but in many ways it's the attitude that's more important. This can be summed up in a single word: curiosity. Moreover, in the words of L. Michael Hall, it's a '*passionate* and *ferocious* curiosity'. We would also add *relentless* to that list. Having an NLP attitude involves wanting to 'see inside other people' and wondering how they come to behave the way they do. It involves questioning, challenging, searching, and not taking anything at face value. The question that most epitomizes an NLP attitude is, 'How do you know?'

When it comes to techniques, NLP has produced some of the most powerful patterns ever devised for facilitating change in people. Some, like the Fast Phobia Cure, are well known, and often when discussion turns to NLP it's the techniques that are mentioned first. But, as John Grinder makes plain, they are the product of NLP's attitude and methodology – the result of modelling and inquiry.

Following their modelling of Perls and Satir, Bandler and Grinder went on to model Milton H. Erickson, the world's foremost medical hypnotist. The result was a different set of language patterns, the Milton Model, and the publication of the second NLP book, *Patterns of the Hypnotic Techniques of Milton H. Erickson MD*.

2

the presuppositions of NLP

At the core of NLP are a dozen or so 'presuppositions' – simple, proverb-like statements such as 'You cannot not communicate' and 'If one person can do something, anyone can learn to do it'. These presuppositions form a semi-coherent philosophy that acts as a set of guiding principles.

Curiously – and perhaps surprisingly – it is not claimed that NLP presuppositions are true, only that they are useful ways of engaging with the world. When your mindset on tackling something new is 'There's no such thing as failure only feedback', for instance, you don't worry so much about making mistakes. You see them as an opportunity to learn, and don't feel you have to do it perfectly first time.

Understanding, embracing and living the NLP presuppositions can have a powerful and liberating effect on your life.

The presuppositions of NLP

When formulating NLP, Richard Bandler and John Grinder drew upon a diverse range of disciplines, including systems theory, cybernetics, transformational grammar, general semantics and logical positivism, not to mention the many fields of therapy they studied. In doing so they embraced many of the underlying concepts of these various approaches, which they synthesized into what came to be known as the 'presuppositions' of NLP.

What does it mean for something to be a 'presupposition'? When we presuppose something we take it as given, accepted without proof, and this is the situation here. In fact, it's not even claimed that NLP presuppositions are true – although there is plenty of evidence to back many of them up. What's considered more important is that they're 'useful', that operating from them leads you to achieving your outcomes.

The map is not the territory

This metaphor is at the heart of NLP. In the same way that a menu is not a meal, and an orchestral score is not a piece of music, so the experience we have of the world is not the world itself. The 'map' is your mind, or own perception, and the 'territory' is reality, the physical world that exists independently of your experience of it. Many people believe their internal map to be a true representation of reality, when in fact it's merely one interpretation.

Everyone lives in their own unique model of the world

We tend to think other people are like us, but given that 'the map is not the territory', it follows that each of us must have our own unique internal model of the world, which is why there is so much variation in the ways individuals behave and think. If you reflect for a moment on some of the people you know or who work with you, you'll be able to recognize how their approach may differ from yours. One person may think his boss has 'high standards' while another thinks of him as 'fussy about detail'. How we react in any given situation is based on our subjective perceptions.

Experience has a structure

NLP is based on the premise that experience has a structure – that the distinctions we make through our five senses, the ways in which we filter and pattern reality, and how we 'code' things such as time, emotions and memories in our brains and bodies are not random, but coherently and systematically organized. Once you understand the way someone is structuring their experience you can help them make changes.

Life, mind and body are one system

While we tend to think of ourselves as separate, autonomous individuals, in reality 'no man is an island'. Leading NLP developer Robert Dilts expresses this elegantly when he says, 'Our bodies, our societies and universe form an ecology of complex systems and sub-systems all of which interact with and mutually influence each other'.

Life, mind and body are one system is one of the central NLP presuppositions because it's important to understand that it's not possible to isolate just one part of a system. Equally, when you change one aspect of a system, you will have in some way changed the rest. People inevitably affect each other by their actions and will be affected by what others do. When working on your own issues, or with other people, you need to be aware of the wider systems that will be involved.

The meaning of a communication is the response you get

Have you ever had the experience of saying or doing something you thought was innocuous or harmless, yet the response you got was unexpected, surprising, and perhaps seemed to you out of all proportion? That's because the message we intend to communicate is not always the one that others receive. What seems acceptable from our 'map' may not be to others. There are two main reasons.

The first is that your communications are channelled through the unique perceptual filters others have, which means their own 'stuff' comes into play. So if someone is sensitive to people who shout, it won't matter what you say if you speak in a loud voice, the response will be the same.

The second is that your communication may not be as 'clean' as you think it is. If, for instance, you were giving praise to a member of staff but were offhand in your manner, they might think you were being false and respond accordingly.

You cannot communicate

It's obvious that when you speak you are communicating, but in fact everything you do affects the people around you. Research has shown that more than 70 per cent of communication is non-verbal, that we unconsciously pick up subtle nuances of position, gesture and expression in our interactions with others. And when we do speak, others are as aware of rhythm, tone and inflection as they are the words said. Even silence can be interpreted as having meaning. If you were to look at someone sitting quietly by themself, in just a few seconds you would have distinct impressions about them. Our mind and body are part of the same system, so the thoughts we have affect our physiology, and 'leak' non-verbally. Because *you cannot not communicate* it's essential that you communicate as clearly and as accurately as you can, rather than leaving it to chance.

Underlying every behaviour is a positive intention

It can sometimes be hard to understand why people behave in the often bizarre, destructive ways they do. What would cause someone to drink excessively, sabotage their relationships, or act aggressively towards others? Yet human behaviour, according to NLP, is not random. There is always a purpose, a reason, a 'positive intention' behind it, which arises when the behaviour is first established. Many people, for instance, start to smoke at the age of 14, in order to feel grown up and impress their friends. Many years later, though, they find it hard to stop, because although the situation has changed, the 'part' responsible is still active.

Sometimes the positive intention is far from obvious, and that's because it's operating, as is often the case, out of conscious awareness.

People make the best choices available to them

According to this presupposition, any behaviour, no matter how strange it may seem, was the best choice available to the person at that moment in time, given their life history, knowledge, beliefs and resources, and viewed from their frame of reference. You might regard them as mistaken, misguided or misinformed, and would have done something different in the same situation, perhaps with more effective results. Then again, there are surely times in your life when someone else would have handled things better than you did. The simple fact is that people, yourself included, do the best they can at the time and could probably do better if only they were aware of other options available to them.

There's no such thing as failure – only feedback

When babies are learning to do new things, such as crawl, stand or walk, they have no sense of failure. They simply have a go, and if that doesn't work they have another go, repeating the process until they get what they want. If, when they tried to stand up for the first time and fell down with a bump they decided they had failed, nobody would be able to walk. Instead, they get feedback about what does and doesn't work, and do more of what does work. Yet by the time they get to be adults most people have become less willing to make 'mistakes', less willing to risk 'failure', perhaps because that might lead to them thinking of *themself* as a failure. They seem to expect to do things well immediately, coming to the conclusion they can't do it at all, instead of using each setback as feedback and as a learning opportunity.

This presupposition is one of the most liberating because once you embrace it you can try all of the things you were once afraid of doing. The more 'failures' you have, the more you learn. So one strategy for learning might be to 'fail' more often!

If what you are doing isn't working, do something else

If you tried a key in a lock and found it wouldn't open, what would you do? Keep trying the same key in the same lock, over and over again? Amazingly, that's what many of us do in certain areas of our lives, like a fly continually hitting itself against a pane of glass in an effort to get outside when there's a gap just inches away. Instead you'd try another key or another lock until you found a combination that works. 'If you always do what you've always done', as the saying goes, 'you'll always get what you've always got'. Flexibility is an essential component of getting the result you want. If you try one way of tackling a problem and don't get the required results, have a go at something different, and keep varying your behaviour until you get the response you're after.

We have the resources within us to achieve what we want

Have you ever heard the expression, 'I didn't know he had it in him'? Many of us are limited by what we believe it's possible for us to achieve and are then surprised when we pull it off. This presupposition asserts that people can bring about change or achieve their outcomes by using the rich pool of inner resources they already have available inside, built up from a lifetime's experience. All that's needed is to access these resources at appropriate times and places. If there is a problem to be solved it could be that an approach you took when tackling something else provides you with the perfect solution.

If one person can do something, anyone can learn to do it

This presupposition encourages us to extend our performance and break through the barriers of what we believe might be possible for us. It's not only a fear of failure that holds us back, it's also our sense of our own limits. But our perceived limits are not our actual limits, and in reality we have virtually infinite potential. While it's not absolutely true to say that if one person can do something, anyone can do it – there are sometimes physical, practical or psychological reasons why that may not be possible – the spirit of the presupposition remains powerful.

People work perfectly

People who have issues such as phobias, social problems or simply don't do something the way they would like to are often thought of as being 'faulty' or 'defective' in some way. But that's not the way in which NLP views things: no one is 'wrong' or 'broken', people work perfectly. So if someone is hopeless at following directions, for instance, the NLP perspective would be that they're good at getting lost or finding a different path to take. Of course, this may not be the outcome they have in mind, in which case it may be necessary to examine things like their strategies and beliefs so they can be more effective.

In any system the person with the most flexibility will control the system

This presupposition derives from systems thinking, where it is known as the Law of Requisite Variety. The word 'control' perhaps overstates the situation; there are sometimes other factors at play, and a better way of expressing the sentiment is 'the person with the greatest flexibility has the best chance of achieving what they want'. Flexibility gives you more options.

Choice is better than no choice

Richard Bandler, one of the originators of NLP, once said, 'The whole point of NLP is having more choice' and many of the presuppositions, along with most of the techniques, relate to increasing the number of choices available in any given situation. Having just one choice is no choice at all. That's what happens with a phobia: every time you see a spider you panic, you don't feel you have any other choice. The more choices you have, the more freedom you have to be in the driving seat of your life.

3

representational systems and submodalities

We take in the world through our five senses and, using the information we gather, we create an internal representation of the world. In NLP these are called representational systems – commonly shortened to 'rep' systems. Much of the time we're engaging with our internal representation of the world, not the world itself.

To confuse matters further, the senses are also known as 'modalities' and also referred to as VAKOG: Visual (seeing), Auditory (hearing), Kinaesthetic (feeling), Olfactory (smelling) and Gustatory (tasting).

Each of the sensory modalities has finer distinctions called submodalities. The sounds we hear in our head, for example, vary in volume, tonality and location, while the images of our internal world vary in brightness, colour, size and so on.

These differences are not random. They are the way we code our experience. When you change the submodalities of an experience, you change the way you feel about it.

When you're sitting in a restaurant enjoying a meal, your senses are being bombarded with stimulation. You smell the food, the perfume of the people you're with, the flowers on the table. You hear the sound of people chattering, of plates and glasses being rattled, of cars passing by outside. You see the room, the customers and staff, and everything on the table. You taste the food, the wine, and if you smoke, perhaps a cigarette. You feel your weight on the seat, the knife and fork in your hand and, towards the end of the meal, a 'full' sensation.

We take in the world through our five senses or, as they are often called in NLP, modalities. That's how we know what's happening around us. There's no other way. Our neurological system then uses the information gathered from our eyes, nose, ears, mouth and the nerve endings in our skin to create an internal representation of the world. It's not a true, complete representation of reality and never could be, because our senses are relatively poor instruments, and can only take in data across a limited range.

We can only pick up sounds, for instance, from 20 Hz to 20,000 Hz, yet many animals can hear well outside that range, and with far greater sensitivity in respect of volume. What we can take in with our eyes is only a narrow part of the spectrum – unlike bats and other creatures, we can't 'see' in the dark. And it's a similar story when it comes to smell, taste and feeling.

But our internal representation is all we have, and we use it as the basis for all aspects of our mental processing as if it were the world itself. Because we use our sensory modalities, working with our neurology, to create this internal representation, they are called *representational systems* in NLP.

The representational systems are often referred to collectively as VAKOG, which is shorthand for: visual (seeing); auditory (hearing); kinaesthetic (feeling and touching); olfactory (smelling); gustatory (tasting). In NLP, most emphasis is placed on visual, auditory and kinaesthetic since they're the ones that are most essential to us in everyday life.

As we think about the world around us, we do so using pictures, sounds, feelings, tastes and smells.

When asked to recall a meeting you attended last week you bring to mind an image of the room or the people who participated. Maybe you remember what someone said – you hear the sound of their voice. Perhaps the weather was cold or the heating too warm. And there might have been a musty smell or tasty food.

Imagine taking the holiday of your dreams. Where will you be going? What will you see when you first arrive? What sounds will you hear? How will it feel to finally visit this place? When we think about the future we use our senses to create mental pictures, sounds and sensations. The world we create inside our heads can be as vivid as the world around us.

Primary system

Although people use all the representational systems available to them, they tend to favour one in particular, 'naturally' thinking in pictures, sounds or feelings. Some individuals find it easy to 'visualize', to see what happened in a memory or construct an image of what could transpire in the future. Others are great at recalling the tune of a piece of music or making up conversations in their mind. And some people are very aware of their feelings. We, of course, use all of the senses to some extent on a daily basis.

The representational system someone uses most of the time is known as their primary, or preferred system. It's normally highly developed, and capable of more discrimination than the other systems. As we grow up we develop an unconscious preference for a particular system and normally by our teens we have a visual, auditory or kinaesthetic disposition. Socialization can play an important role. If as children we spend several years learning to play a musical instrument, the auditory modality may come to the fore. Ballet or martial arts will help strengthen the kinaesthetic sense. And painting will do the same for the visual modality. Playing computer games is likely to develop both visual sophistication and kinaesthetic dexterity.

Predicates

Although we're not aware of it, the words and phrases we use indicate the representational system we're using at any one time. When someone declares they 'can see the light at the end of the tunnel', you know they're processing visually. When your boss 'likes the sound' of your idea, it's an auditory modality in operation. And when your friend wants you to 'grasp the nettle', you know they're thinking kinaesthetically.

If you listen carefully to someone speaking for even a short while you'll notice a pattern in the kinds of words and phrases they choose that reflects either their primary system or the particular context they're involved with.

Visual

Appear, bird's-eye view, catch a glimpse of, clarify, clear-cut, dark, dress up, enlighten, examine, expose, focus, glance, glimpse, graphic, hazy idea, hindsight, illusion, illustrate, in light of, in view of, look, look into it, make a scene, mind's eye, notice, obvious, outlook, perspective, picture, pinpoint, reveal, see, short-sighted, spectacle, take a dim view, tunnel vision, under your nose, vague.

Auditory

Audible, call, clear as a bell, clearly expressed, compose, discuss, earful, earshot, harmonize, hear, hidden message, listen, loud and clear, manner of speaking, mention, note, outspoken, remark, report, say, scream, shout, silence, sing, sound, speechless, tell the truth, tongue-tied, tune-in, voice, well informed, word for word.

Kinaesthetic

Affected, bear, boils down to, carry, cold, cool, crash, crawl, emotional, foundation, get a load of this, get in touch with, grab, grip, handle, hang in there, hassle, heated, hold, hot-headed, impact, irritate, lay cards on the table, lukewarm, motion, muddled, nail, pressure, rub, shallow, sharpen, shift, shock, slipped my mind, solid, sore, stir, stress, strike, tap, throw, tickle, tied up, touch, wring.

All the above include words that are known as predicates, sensory-based process words in the form of nouns, verbs, adjectives and adverbs. During the next few days pay attention to what people say. Notice how many predicates relating to a particular representational system they use. You may find it easier to listen to people on the radio, that way you won't be distracted by any visual input.

Matching predicates

The great value of knowing someone's primary representational system is that you can use it when communicating with them. It enhances communication enormously because you are literally 'speaking their language', the language they use to think.

What do you observe about this exchange?

A	Can you give me a hand? I'm having trouble grasping these concepts, they're very hard.
B	I'll see what I can do to clarify things. Hopefully I'll have a bright idea.

You probably noticed that A is using kinaesthetic language and B is responding with visual language, which may hinder communication. A better response might have been:

B	Just hang in there, I'll get to grips with it and try to get things moving.

Using the same modality of sensory-based predicates the other person favours, irrespective of your primary system, is extremely effective in rapport terms. If you're unsure about what predicates to use, either because you've only just met the person, or there's a group of people, mix in visual, auditory and kinaesthetic expressions. That way you'll appeal to everyone.

Lead system

Since our primary representational system is our preferred system, you might have expected we'd all use it for every aspect of conscious processing. In fact, though, some of us have a separate 'lead' system for bringing things into awareness, whether they're from the external environment or generated internally.

Bringing to mind a memory is a good way to check what your 'lead' system is. Do you get a picture, sound or feeling first? Try it with a few memories, some recent, some when you were younger. If it's always the same modality, that's your lead system. What's important to understand is that it's not the full representation, just the key that unlocks the door. For every memory, or visualization, you normally have a full VAKOG representation stored internally. And the way you gain access to it is by first seeing a picture, hearing a sound, having a feeling, or experiencing a smell or taste.

Eye accessing cues

The quickest and easiest way of discovering someone's lead system is by watching their eyes carefully when you ask them a question. You may have thought eye movements are random or, more likely, never thought about them at all – but in fact they clearly indicate the representational system someone is using at any one time. And as the modality changes, so does the direction in which the eye looks.

These eye accessing cues, as they are known – 'cue' in this context meaning a signal that something is happening – are virtually universal. While many people have the pattern opposite, there are individual differences – in left-handed people, for instance, the pattern may be reversed.

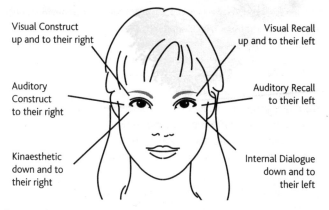

Visual Construct
up and to their right

Visual Recall
up and to their left

Auditory
Construct
to their right

Auditory Recall
to their left

Kinaesthetic
down and to
their right

Internal Dialogue
down and to
their left

Eye accessing cues. NB. Diagram shows eye accessing cues for a right-handed person as you see them.

People look up when they're processing visually. When they look up to their left they're recalling a picture they've seen before, such as their front door. When they look up and to their right they're constructing an image they haven't seen before, such as a pink tiger with yellow stripes.

When people's eyes move directly to their left they're recalling a sound they've heard before, such as their boss's voice, and when they look to their right they're hearing an unfamiliar or constructed sound, perhaps a melody they're making up.

When someone looks down to their left they're listening to their own internal dialogue. Most of us experience an internal voice – it can be like having your own running commentary on life. When people look down to their right they're in touch with their feelings.

What are submodalities?

By now you're familiar with the five representational systems – visual, auditory, kinaesthetic, olfactory and gustatory – but this is only part of the story. For each of the sensory modalities there are finer details and distinctions, which are known as submodalities.

When we're thinking visually, for instance, the pictures in our mind's eye have colour, brightness, contrast, depth, size and so on. Sounds have volume, location, tonality, etc. The feelings within our body have temperature, intensity, duration and more. The same is true of our olfactory and gustatory senses.

Submodalities are the way we code and make up the structure of our internal experience. As with so many other things, most of the time this happens outside of our conscious awareness. Every thought we have, whether a memory or vision of the future, is formed out of these nuances of pictures, sounds, feelings, tastes and smells.

How submodalities function

The best way – arguably the *only* way – to understand how submodalities function is to experience them. And to do that you need to engage with your own experience.

So, allow yourself to think back to a time when you were relaxed and happy, perhaps on holiday. Tune into the visual element of your memory and, looking through your own eyes, recall what you saw at the time. Is your image in colour or black and white? Is it moving or still? Is it panoramic or is there a frame around it like a picture? How far away or near to you is it? Does it have a specific location? You may find you can make more distinctions than this.

Now play around with it. As you look at your image turn up the brightness. Does it alter how you feel about it? Then gradually make the image dimmer until you can barely make it out. Many people find there's an optimum brightness at which their feelings intensify, and when it's too light or dark they don't have any feelings for it at all.

If the image is moving, make it frozen, like a postcard. If it's already still, give it movement. How does that change things? If it's colour turn it to black and white, and if it's already monochromatic, fill it with colour. What's the effect? Move your mental image further away, then closer, to the side, and up and down. How do you feel when it's in those different locations?

Now tune into the auditory element of your memory and recall what you heard at the time. What sounds are you aware of – voices, music or a noise of some kind? How many sound sources are there? Are the sounds close by or some distance away? Which direction do the sounds come from? Do they sound as clear as a bell or are any of them muffled? If there are voices are they pitched high or low? Are they speaking quickly or slowly?

Try turning up the volume and get a sense of the difference it makes to your experience. Now turn it down to a whisper. If there are a number of voices or sounds adjust the tone of each one, much like you would if you were using a graphic equalizer. Move the sounds around into different locations. Try changing the speed. What effect do each of these changes have on the way you feel about it?

Finally, get in touch with any feelings you experienced at the time. Where in your body were they? How would you describe the sensations? Were they strong or weak? Diffused or focused? What happens if you move them around or change their intensity?

What you've just done is to briefly experience the 'fabric' of your submodalities – how they're made up. You may have been surprised when you started changing the way your memory was coded, that it could have such a significant effect. Most people have never thought of altering the brightness of an internal image or the volume of an internal sound to feel differently about things.

What you were doing was changing your internal representation, and you can do it with any memory, 'good' or 'bad', strengthening those which you value and weakening those which cause you problems. You can also use the same process when planning what you want to do in the future. By optimizing the submodalities, you can make your 'outcomes' compelling.

Recognizing submodalities

To recognize submodalities all you need to know is what to look for. You can practise by describing an everyday experience in detail and check the list below to find out how you've coded your experience.

Typical submodalities

Visual representations
Associated – dissociated
Moving – still
Framed – panoramic
Foreground or background contrast
Horizontal or vertical perspective
Location of image
Dull – bright
Black and white – colour
Colour balance
Fast – slow – still
Distance: near – far
Clear – blurred
Three-dimensional – flat or two-dimensional
Shape
Size

Auditory representations
Stereo – mono
Location of sounds
Volume: loud – soft
Tone: bass – treble
Pitch: high – low
Tempo: fast – slow
Close – far
Rhythm
Melody
Quality: clear – muffled
Continuous – discontinuous
Soft – harsh
Number of sound sources
Kind of sound: music, voice – whose voice?

Kinaesthetic representations

Constant – intermittent
Location of sensations – internal or external
Strong – weak
Large area – small area
Texture: rough – smooth
Dry – wet
Temperature: hot – cold
Pressure and weight: heavy – light
Still – moving
Rhythm – regular or irregular
Intensity

Auditory digital representations (internal voice)

Sensory based or evaluative
About self or others
Current – past – future
Location of words
Volume
Pitch
Simple or complex

Analogue and digital submodalities

There are two main types of submodalities, digital and analogue. Digital submodalities are either on or off. A mental picture, for instance, is either moving or still. There are no intermediate positions. Analogue submodalities, on the other hand, are infinitely variable between the extremes. Sounds vary along a continuum between quiet and loud. The majority of submodalities are analogue, with just a handful that are digital.

The value of submodalities

You may be wondering how knowing about submodalities might be of use to you. In fact it's extremely valuable, because it allows you to choose the way you code your memories and dreams for the future. And in doing so you can alter their meaning and make them more or less memorable, desirable, credible or intense.

Creating change with submodalities

The impact and meaning of a memory is affected more by the submodalities used to code it than the actual content. Once something's taken place it's impossible to change what actually happened, but what can be altered is the way the experience is coded. This alters the meaning of our internal representation of the original event, and how we feel about it. The desired outcome of many NLP patterns is either to diminish or amplify the intensity of a remembered experience.

Many people have memories that are unpleasant and uncomfortable, and which cause them problems in the here and now. There might have been a traumatic incident or some other kind of significant emotional experience. The result is a phobia, a panic attack, or an irrational fear that is debilitating and makes life difficult.

What happens is that when we recall the event or something happens to trigger a memory of it, the emotion comes flooding back. Since the event itself is in the past, what's causing the problem has to be the way it's been coded into memory. And that's largely down to the submodality distinctions. By changing crucial details of the coding, it's possible for the intense emotion to be drained from a memory, and for the person never to be troubled by it again.

Contrastive analysis

One of the most useful techniques in working with submodalities is contrastive analysis, which can be used to find 'the difference that makes the difference' between two states or internal representations. Contrastive analysis is used in many NLP processes and is especially useful where one experience gives a desirable outcome and the other produces undesirable results.

If we experience one memory as emotional and one as neutral, there must be a difference in the way they are coded. By identifying the submodalities that are different – the *critical* submodalities – it's possible to effect a change, quickly and easily.

Mapping across

Because the way in which we experience a memory depends primarily on the way it's coded, changing the submodalities of an unpleasant memory to those of a pleasant memory will mean it becomes, as far as our neurological system is concerned, a pleasant experience.

The process by which this is achieved in NLP is called Mapping Across. It simply involves 'copying and pasting' the submodalities that are different from the pleasant to the unpleasant memory. This is normally done one at a time, until what had been the unpleasant memory has exactly the same submodalities as the pleasant memory. Although it may sound complicated, or difficult, it's actually straightforward.

The driver submodality

Sometimes, as you transfer the submodalities, you'll change one and many others will change at the same time. This is called the driver submodality, and it is the most 'critical' of the critical submodalities. It's like a master switch that controls all the others. This is sometimes referred to as 'the domino effect'. There's not always a driver, but if you encounter one you don't need to complete the mapping across process – in a sense the job has been done for you.

4

values and beliefs

The importance of beliefs and values in NLP cannot be overstated because they provide the driving, motivating force behind behaviour. You might think of them as the 'rules we live by' – the 'shoulds', 'musts' and 'have tos' that determine what we do, what we buy, what we think, and so on.

Many beliefs and values operate out of conscious awareness, and we're not aware of the degree to which they guide our behaviour, shape our personality and define our identity.

Some of the beliefs we have are empowering, but many are limiting – they prevent us doing what we want and achieving our goals. Beliefs and values are, though, learnt – and that means they can be changed if they don't give us what we want.

Children are often told they can't dance, sing, draw (the list goes on) and come to believe this to be true. But once they 'break the spell' and realize, as adults, that dancing, singing, drawing, etc. are skills that can be learnt, a new, more useful belief can be 'installed'.

6 May 1954 marked a turning point in world athletics. Up to that date it was believed to be impossible for anyone to run a mile in under four minutes. No one had ever achieved it. The last time the record had been broken was in 1945, and it stood resolutely at 4:01:4. But one man, Roger Bannister, a 25-year-old medical student from Harrow, believed it was possible – and on that date he proved it, crossing the finishing line in a time of 3:59:4. Yet within 46 days, his great rival John Landy, whose best time thus far had been 1.5 seconds outside the four-minute barrier, ran even faster than Bannister, recording a time of 3:57:9. And over the next three years, 16 runners were to log sub-four-minute miles.

We may not be planning to beat a world record, but beliefs play a crucial role in all our lives. If we believe something is possible we may seek to achieve it. If we believe it's impossible we probably won't even try. Once Roger Bannister had made the four-minute mile a reality, others were able to believe they could do it. They broke through their psychological barriers and, literally, followed in his footsteps.

Beliefs are not trivial, unimportant things. People are willing to die, and kill, for them. When, on 11 September 2001, two American aeroplanes were hijacked and flown into the Twin Towers that dominated the New York skyline, razing them to the ground, it was a belief in something more important than life that motivated those responsible. And when President George Bush responded by attacking Afghanistan and then Iraq, his actions were underpinned by an unswerving and absolute belief that terrorism must be defeated whatever the cost.

Understanding beliefs and values

In *Unlimited Power*, Anthony Robbins defines a belief as 'Any guiding principle, dictum, faith, or passion that can provide meaning and direction in life'. Beliefs are, then, assumptions and presuppositions we have about ourselves, other people, and the world in general.

Our beliefs arise within a specific cultural setting, and are often shared by others in our family and social circle. As a result they are invisible much of the time. We take them for granted and, more importantly, accept them as true. It's typically only when we encounter someone who has a different set of beliefs that we become aware of our own.

'Pure' beliefs are largely emotionless. You believe them but they evoke no feelings. You believe the sun will set at the end of the day. You believe your house will continue standing. It's no big deal, it's just the way things are. Some beliefs, though, are also judgements about the way things should be. These are called values, because they imply an evaluation.

'Values,' says Anthony Robbins, 'are private, personal, individual beliefs about what is most important to you. Your values are belief systems about right, wrong, good, and bad.' Values, then, are a guiding principle, an internal compass, by which we live our lives, shaping the kinds of experiences we seek out and those we avoid.

The power of beliefs

There's considerable evidence for the power of beliefs across a range of fields, but the Placebo Effect is probably the most compelling. Placebos are pills containing sugar or starch, or liquids containing no active agents. Yet research has shown time and again that a significant proportion of patients who are given placebos believe them to be therapeutic and actually get well. The success rate varies according to the situation, but placebos are typically as effective as real drugs in over one-third of cases.

In one study, patients suffering pain from a wisdom tooth extraction got as much relief from a fake application of ultrasound as a real one. And warts that had proved resistant to other treatments were successfully eliminated when they were painted using a brightly coloured, inert dye, with the promise that they would be gone once the colour wore off. They were.

Such studies show clearly that our beliefs can determine the way things turn out. They're not mere 'thoughts', they're instructions. Believing something sends a psycho-neurological message through your entire mind/body system that seeks to make it happen.

The language of beliefs and values

The expressions people use often reveal their beliefs and values. The words 'can' and 'can't' in particular are a clear indication of a belief. The same is true when ideas are presented dogmatically, with no room for debate. When beliefs are deeply held, they often lead to black and white thinking. Words such as 'right' and 'wrong', 'appropriate' and 'inappropriate', 'good' and 'bad', 'should' and 'shouldn't', and 'important' and 'unimportant' tell you immediately that someone is talking in terms of their values.

Beliefs change

Beliefs and values are not fixed. We often act as if they are facts when in reality they are only our perceptions. They may guide our thinking and our behaviour, and we may hold on to some of them for long periods, but they can and do change naturally over time. When you were five, for example, you probably thought Father Christmas and the Easter Bunny were real.

Limiting beliefs

Beliefs can be positive driving forces in people's lives but they can also be disempowering and limiting. When Emma started to learn to play the piano she found she couldn't play a tune fluently straight away and became disheartened. She began to think of it as difficult and told other people she would never be able to play well. Not long after she gave up.

Many of us had the experience at school of being told by a teacher that we couldn't draw, sing, dance or whatever. We believed them, and stopped trying. Yet a moment's reflection will reveal those beliefs to be untrue. We can all draw, sing and dance to a degree, though admittedly not as well as Michelangelo, Pavarotti and Nureyev. 'People can, and do,' observes L. Michael Hall, 'believe all kinds of utterly idiotic things.'

One of the reasons that we don't realize our beliefs are illogical is that they're largely self-fulfilling. When you believe something, you act in a way that validates it. That's true whether it's a positive or negative belief. The life we create and the experiences we have are determined to a significant degree by what we believe. When we believe we can't do something, our behaviour will be such that we 'fail', perhaps by not trying hard enough or by sabotaging ourselves in some way.

Understanding values

The importance of values cannot be overstated. Just imagine what it would be like if nothing mattered to you. Why would you want to do anything? What would be the point? People who have a strong sense of what's important to them usually have a real sense of purpose that acts like a propulsion system, which moves them towards it.

Stop and think for a minute. All the things you want to do are ways of actualizing your values. At the highest level, these are likely to be things such as security, making a difference, independence, living life to the full, acceptance and helping others. Values are essentially generalizations about what does or doesn't matter. And behaviour flows directly from them. If someone values fairness, for instance, they may also believe that people should treat one another equally, and act that way themself. If they don't follow up with this behaviour they feel uncomfortable with their actions.

In his book *First Things First*, Stephen Covey advocates using your personal values as the basis for how you allocate your time, being guided, as he puts it, by the compass rather than the clock. By this he means prioritizing based on your personal mission, vision and values – what's most important to you.

5

well-formed outcomes

We all have goals: things we want to have, things we want to do. Some we achieve quickly and easily. Others take longer and are more challenging. Some seem to be downright impossible.

But what if you had a set of steps that increased the likelihood of achieving those goals? That's what the NLP 'Well-Formed Outcomes' model promises. Follow the steps and you're virtually guaranteed success – as well as accelerating your progress.

All too often the goals we set ourselves are woolly or depend on other people, and it's no wonder they fall by the wayside or wither on the vine.

By creating outcomes that meet a series of 'Well-formedness' conditions – such as stating them in the positive and being as specific as possible – you take account of the way the brain works when considering options, pursuing goals and being motivated, which means you increase the likelihood of achieving them.

'Well-formed' outcomes

In business, people often use SMART – an acronym for Specific, Measurable, Achievable, Realistic and Time-bound – to sharpen up their goals. This is a valuable and worthwhile process, but has its limitations. Goals can still end up fuzzy and not fully thought through. In NLP, it's considered essential that outcomes be 'well-formed', that is, they meet a series of rigorous criteria or 'conditions' designed to increase the likelihood of their success. These are:

1 State the outcome in positive terms.
2 Ensure the outcome is within your control.
3 Be as specific as possible.
4 Have a sensory-based evidence procedure.
5 Consider the context.
6 Have access to resources.
7 Ensure the outcome preserves existing benefits.
8 Check the outcome is ecologically sound.
9 Define the first step.

Let's take a look at them all now in depth.

1 State the outcome in positive terms

Many people express their goals in negative terms: 'I don't want to smoke', 'I don't want to feel nervous when presenting', 'I don't want to worry about the future'. But there's a problem with this way of thinking because of how our minds work. When we use negative language we end up focusing on what we don't want, which has the opposite effect to what was intended.

If someone says 'Don't think of a guitar', the only way you can remember not to think of it is to think of it. You have to hold it in your mind and then cancel or delete it. For that reason, NLP insists that all outcomes are stated in positive terms. So 'I don't want to feel nervous when I'm presenting' is revised to 'I want to feel confident when I present', on which the mind can focus without distraction.

2 Ensure the outcome is within your control

It's also essential that the outcome is under your control. If it requires other people to do certain things, or not do certain things,

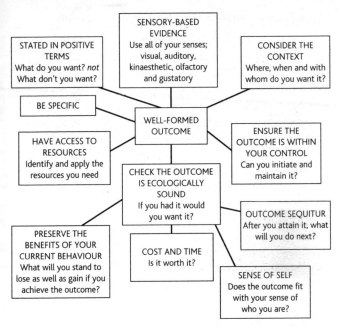

Well-formed outcomes.

it's not an acceptable outcome in NLP terms. The problem with the outcome, 'I want my daughter to do well at college' is that it's not totally under the person's control. It's dependent on the action of other people. 'I want to provide reading materials to support my daughter's education', or 'I will help my daughter in every way possible' are both outcomes that are well formed in this regard.

3 Be as specific as possible

Many outcomes are vague and woolly, such as 'I want to do something interesting' or 'I want to be rich'. NLP requires that outcomes be defined in sensory specific language, that is in terms of what can be seen, heard and felt. When we refine an outcome by clarifying the detail the whole thing becomes more vivid and real. The more specific we are the less likelihood there is of ending up with something we don't want.

4 Have a sensory-based evidence procedure

This well-formedness condition is linked to the last one. Having defined your outcome as specifically as possible, you need to put in place a sensory-based evidence procedure. If you were working with someone else, you would ask them, 'How will you know when you've achieved your goal?' and expect the answer to be in terms of what someone would see, hear, feel, taste or smell. This degree of specificity is required because people often have evidence procedures that are abstract, and as with many things, 'the devil is in the detail'.

5 Consider the context

It's also essential to consider where, when and with whom the outcome is wanted. Does it relate to the whole of their life or just part of it? An outcome that works well in one context may not fit in another. Someone may want more challenges at work and more relaxation at home.

If someone wants to be honest and direct, do they want it in every situation? With their boss? With their partner? All the time? That sounds like a recipe for conflict. Perhaps the context in which the behaviour will operate needs to be specified more clearly. And the people involved. One useful question is, 'When don't I want this outcome?' This will allow appropriate boundaries to be established.

6 Have access to resources

One of the goals of NLP is to support people in moving from their 'current state' to a 'desired state'. To achieve this they usually need 'resources'. These may be internal, such as skills, knowledge, understanding and courage, or external, such as money, contacts or equipment.

If, for instance, the outcome was to run a marathon, what resources do they have, what can they do already? Perhaps they regularly run ten miles. They've got quality footwear that can take the extra pounding. They have a friend who wants to do it as well, and will train with them. And so on.

What resources are they lacking? Well, they've never before actually run 26 miles. But two years ago they completed a 40-mile walk, and that confidence can be transferred to support the latest outcome. They don't know enough about 'pasta loading', which is supposed to help sustain energy, and they need to find out.

7 Ensure the outcome preserves existing benefits

Many people are motivated and committed to achieving an outcome yet still don't attain it or it doesn't last. This is often because their current behaviour provides benefits that will be lost if they accomplish what they set out to do. In NLP, such benefits are known as 'positive by-products' or 'secondary gains'.

8 Check the outcome is ecological

NLP places great importance on 'ecology', on taking into account the effect of any change to the wider systems of which a person is part. Each outcome we set and achieve, no matter how small, will create a ripple effect on the world around us and the people in it.

Ecology is about the consequences for the system as a whole. And this well-formedness condition involves thinking carefully and deeply about the advantages and disadvantages in following any course of action.

Do you want the outcome no matter the price? Maybe you want to be better qualified to improve your career prospects. Are you prepared to spend six years studying for an Open University degree and to invest several hundred pounds a year doing it?

There are four classic NLP questions that cover the important ecology issues:

* What will happen if you achieve this outcome?
* What won't happen if you achieve this outcome?
* What will happen if you don't achieve this outcome?
* What won't happen if you don't achieve this outcome?

9 Define the first step

Turning an outcome into reality requires action. And even the longest journey begins, as an ancient proverb says, with a single step. Defining that first step is a final and important part of the well-formedness process. If you don't take that step, you probably won't take the others that follow afterwards. Once again, be specific: what precisely will you do, and when will you do it?

6

states, emotions and anchoring

NLP places great emphasis on 'state' – the way you're feeling at any moment in time. That's because the state you're in affects how you think, how you behave, and the results you get.

When you're feeling 'resourceful' – confident, positive, energetic – you try new things, tackle them with vigour and often succeed. When you're feeling 'unresourceful' – uncertain, negative, lethargic – often you struggle.

But with NLP it's possible to choose your state – one that will be useful for the situation you find yourself in. And you can choose it at will, using a range of techniques.

Anchoring is an NLP term for an association. We hear a piece of music (auditory anchor) and recall a wonderful evening with a loved one. We see a snake (visual anchor) and have a phobic reaction because we were startled by one when younger. Anything we can see, hear, feel, taste or smell (the five modalities) can be an anchor.

The state we're in

In everyday conversation it's not unusual to describe someone as being in a 'state' of some kind – a state of panic, a state of boredom, a state of bliss. The term is also used in a more general way: 'he's in a right old state', 'look at the state of her'.

Tony Robbins suggests that state is the 'sum of the millions of neurological processes happening within us – the sum total of our experience – at any one time'. In short, it's a heady cocktail of everything that's going on in the body and the mind.

In a typical day most of us go through a range of states, some of which we experience as positive and enjoyable (happiness, love, pleasure, confidence), and others which seem negative and unpleasant (frustration, tiredness, anger, sadness). Some are fleeting, lasting just a few seconds or minutes. Others are more enduring, and we have them for most of the day, or even longer. Our state is constantly changing. Not all states have names. Sometimes we're just 'in a good mood' or we 'feel out of sorts'. On other occasions we feel as if we got out of the wrong side of the bed. Nothing goes right. The whole world's against us. Other times we can't put a foot wrong. Everything we touch turns to gold.

Mostly, though, we're somewhere in-between, until something happens to change it. For many people life is like a roller-coaster. Sometimes they're up, sometimes they're down, as their feelings get tossed around by the experiences life throws at them. Their boss either gives them a hard time because they haven't completed a task, or praise for a job they did well, and they feel lousy or elated.

What would it be like if you could choose your state, rather than have it controlled by what happens to you? Well, with NLP that's possible. It's simply a matter of using your brain in a way that gives you what you want.

Behaviour arises from state

The state we're in is important because it not only affects how we feel, it also determines how we behave and our ability to perform well. When we feel confident, we act with boldness. When we feel apprehensive, we act timidly. When we're in a 'negative', unresourceful state, we struggle with things we find easy to accomplish when we're feeling strong and resourceful. Although we're still the same person, our state makes all the difference.

Have you ever tried to do something, such as write a report or find the solution to a problem, and found it virtually impossible, only to have another go later, perhaps after a good night's sleep, and find it easy and effortless? That's the power of state, and one of the reasons certain states are highly sought after. Not only are they enjoyable, they're also empowering.

How we create states

Most of us experience states as 'happening' to us, and think of them as being outside of our control. In fact we create them by the way in which we perceive the world. We're able to choose our state and are able to run our own brain, rather than have it running us.

In NLP, the mind and body are thought of as one system, directly influencing each other, with changes in one impacting on the other. When we alter any aspect of our neurology and physiology, such as rate of breathing, blood pressure, temperature, muscle tension and posture, there's a corresponding variation in our mental state. And the thoughts we have – that is the way in which we represent the world internally – have a powerful influence over our neuro-physiology. It's a cybernetic loop.

When most people look at someone they love or hear a favourite song they get a warm feeling inside. And when they look at an unpleasant photograph or hear footsteps behind them in the street at night the feeling they get is uncomfortable. These are examples of how external stimuli create or change our state.

Changing state

If you like your baseline state, and your other familiar states, there may seem no obvious reason to change them and it may even seem strange to think about doing so. But you can if you want to.

And given the choice wouldn't you rather be in a high performance 'peak' state or a relaxed state?

NLP places great emphasis on being able to manage state, because when you're in the right state for the situation you're more likely to achieve your outcome.

When you see a police car in the rear-view mirror of your car it's likely that you'll slow down or check your speedometer regardless of whether you're driving too fast or not. The image of the police car in the rear-view mirror is, in NLP terminology, an anchor which triggers an automatic behaviour in many of us.

Virtually anything we can remember or perceive can act as an anchor: the smell of freshly baked bread, the memory of a house we used to live in, the touch of a loved one, etc. Many people report that when they hear a piece of music they can recall where they were when they first listened to it, who they were with and how they felt at the time.

The process by which an internal response became paired, or associated with, an external or internal experience is called anchoring. In the same way that a ship's anchor holds the ship in place, an anchor becomes a reference point for a particular experience.

Anchoring is similar to behavioural conditioning, which Pavlov made famous. Over a period of time Pavlov rang a bell when he was about to feed his dogs. He subsequently discovered that if he rang the bell without feeding them they still salivated, indicating that an association had been established. The difference between this stimulus–response concept and the NLP approach is that it takes account of the fact that human beings have a range of mental processes that are more complex.

Everyday anchors

Anchors are naturally occurring. Things we see, hear, feel, taste and touch in our everyday lives spontaneously evoke memories, and often feelings as well. While some anchors are neutral – you see a blue car and it reminds you of one you used to own – many trigger some kind of emotional reaction.

A particular voice tone could remind us of a critical parent. A lake might remind us of a time we nearly drowned. Phobias are examples of extreme 'negative' anchors. A spider, confined space or something equally innocuous has become associated with danger, and produces a fearful response.

Sometimes anchors are set as the result of a single, traumatic experience. But more often, like the bell and Pavlov's dogs, they are established through repetition, and strengthened over time. If every time you went to do something you got shouted at, you would quickly learn not to do it and that association, that anchor, would persist.

Anchors are learned programs and they're state dependent. Pavlov's dogs had to be hungry for the stimulus to have any effect. Many anchors originate in childhood. Often the original experience that created them has long since been forgotten, but the emotional response continues.

Other anchors set off positive feelings. Looking at a photograph from a holiday brings back thoughts of happy times, while holding a brooch that belonged to a grandmother can be a reminder of the smile on her face.

Words, too, are anchors. When we read or hear a word such as 'table' it may bring to mind various tables that we've seen before. Advertising is based on anchors. The aim is to create an association that encourages you to buy certain products. Aftershave may be sold on the basis that men wearing it will be fighting off a host of beautiful admirers.

Using anchoring

Many of the anchored responses we have are useful to us. They allow us to function effectively in the world without having to consciously think too much about what we're doing. We don't have to remember to press our foot on the brake pedal when we see the brake lights on the car in front of us light up. It's an automatic, anchored response. Perhaps you've had the experience of 'braking' when you've been a passenger, and the driver didn't seem to respond quickly enough.

Anchors, though, don't have to be left to chance. You can set them – intentionally, systematically – in support of your desired outcomes. If you want to be in a particular state or feel a specific emotion in a future context, you can create an anchor that achieves that.

Circle of excellence

We all have the resources within us to achieve what we want. The experiences we've had in life are all stored away in our unconscious mind and can be retrieved to support our current endeavours. Circle of Excellence is a technique that allows us to access these resources. You could use it to increase your confidence in public speaking and making presentations, or whatever. The process is most often carried out with two people and can be used on yourself. The version described below doesn't require anyone else's involvement.

Steps
1 Think of a situation where your current or anticipated behaviour does not give you the outcome you want. You may, for instance, have a presentation to do in the next few weeks and want to feel confident.
2 Mentally 'lay down' a circle on the floor wherever you wish. Make it whatever size you like. Give it a colour and a soft humming sound too if you wish. Don't step into it yet.
3 Reflect for a moment on the resources that would be useful to you in the situation you've selected.
4 Recall a time when you had those resources, taking each one in turn. It can be three different times or a single time when you had all of the required resources. You are seeking really good examples of each resource. It's common to have at least three resources and it could be more. If you want to make an effective presentation you might, for instance, choose confidence, feeling calm and clearly articulating a message. Sometimes people can't recall a time when they

had a particular resource. If this happens to you, think of someone you know who has the resource and pretend you're them. You can include the visual anchor of this person in place of your own memory.

5 When you've identified a resource, step into the circle and relive that experience. Taking the example of confidence, vividly recall a time when you were really confident. Relive it, seeing what you saw, hearing what you heard and feeling what you felt. Repeat this process for each named resource, stacking one on top of the other.

6 Think of a specific time in the future when you want to have those resources. If it's confidence in presenting, for instance, see and hear what will be there just before you want to feel confident.

7 Now step back into the circle. Access all those resources, take them to where they're needed, and feel the difference. Imagine the situation in your mind's eye. You can add an additional auditory or kinaesthetic anchor at this stage such as hand clapping or squeezing a finger and thumb together.

8 Step out of the circle again. Now imagine a time in the future when a similar experience may happen and become aware of how different it is with these resources.

9 Finally, test to make sure it has completely worked by recalling the original situation. Check how it feels now. If you have any doubts you may need an additional resource in which case you should repeat the process adding this in.

7

sensory acuity and calibration

Many people seem to 'sleepwalk' through their lives, not really noticing what's going on around them. They're oblivious to others and to the world at large. But if you're not 'tuned in', how can you know if you're getting what you want?

NLP considers 'sensory acuity' to be essential – part of a feedback process that lets you know whether you're moving closer to your goals or further away. Excellent observational skills are also important if you're going to be able to build rapport with others.

Someone with highly developed sensory acuity is able to pick up on changes in skin colour, voice tone and other small nuances in behaviour that reveal a lot about what the other person is thinking and feeling.

The next step is to notice patterns in behaviour – this is called calibration. This can be extremely valuable when playing poker, enabling you to know whether someone is bluffing or not.

Being aware of what's going on around us is essential if we're to be effective in the world, but people vary in how much they take in. Some have highly developed and finely tuned observational skills, and pick up on every detail and nuance. Others seem lost in their own thoughts, and wouldn't even notice if a Yeti walked by carrying the Loch Ness Monster.

Of course, it also depends on what we're doing and how we're feeling. Have you ever driven along a road you know like the back of your hand and missed your turning because your mind was elsewhere? And travelled the same route on a different occasion and been acutely aware of every curve and twist of the landscape.

When taking a holiday in an exotic location our senses come alive as we delight in all the new sights and sounds, tastes and smells. Yet when we're at home we barely look up when we walk down the street. The good news is that we can develop our ability to observe fine detail, known in NLP as 'sensory acuity', through practice and by consciously paying attention to what's happening around you.

How to develop sensory acuity

A good place to start developing your sensory acuity is to become aware of the kind of things you notice already – you might think of it as carrying out a stocktake of your observational skills. The simple act of reflecting on your behaviour will expand your range anyway, because you'll automatically begin to consider what's not on your list that could be.

Another useful way to expand your range is to compare your abilities with other people you know. Do you know people who regularly comment on things they observe in the world around them, or who seem to be good at noticing human behaviour? What do others notice that you don't?

Observation and interpretation

One thing that's really important is to be able to keep your observation 'pure', to prevent it spilling over into interpretation. The starting point is to understand the difference:

* Observation is simply what you notice with your senses: what you see, hear, feel, taste and smell.
* Interpretation is when you go beyond the sensory information gathered and draw a conclusion of some kind.

Once you understand the difference between observation and interpretation, you can go on to do something useful with all the data you'll gather. Which brings us to calibration.

Calibration

We all notice patterns in human behaviour. When the boss walks into the room Bob starts working. Whenever money is mentioned everyone goes quiet. Kate takes a deep breath before she makes important announcements.

In NLP, noticing patterns of behaviour is called calibration, defined by Joseph O'Connor and Ian McDermott as 'Correlating signs you can see and hear with the other person's state'. It's the process of using sensory acuity to pay precise attention to changes in another person's state by detecting patterns in the nuances of their behaviour – the way they breathe, their voice tone or volume, skin colour, micro muscle movement, posture and gestures.

You can forget the 'one-size-fits-all' approach to body language taken by most books on the subject, in which looking away always means you're avoiding the issue. NLP doesn't see things like that at all. Although there are similarities between us, we are each unique individuals with our own pattern of responses. And calibration is the process of identifying the behavioural cues that go with or before a particular state – 'x' always accompanies or precedes 'y'.

The more well developed our calibration skills, the more connections we pick up. This doesn't mean guessing, it's essential you work from sensory specific evidence. If, for instance, you observe on several occasions that someone frowns and narrows their eyes when they don't agree with something, the next time they do those things, even if they don't say anything, you may be able to conclude they disagree.

rapport

One of the precursors of NLP, Milton H. Erickson, famously said: 'Without rapport, nothing is possible. With rapport, everything is possible'. He meant that when you're in rapport with others, you quickly build a connection that enables you to influence and lead them.

How do you build rapport? There are several ways. One of the easiest is to match the other person's body language. You sit or stand like them, move like them and gesture like them. We tend to like people who are like us, and the way we move is an intimate expression of who we are. You can also match someone's voice – its speed, volume, rhythm and overall energy.

For maximum rapport, match the words and expressions people use and find common ground in terms of beliefs and values.

What is rapport?

Have you noticed that when people are in conversation with colleagues at work, chatting over the garden fence or are out together having a drink in a bar they often adopt similar poses and postures? They make eye contact, chat easily, and are comfortable in each other's company. Perhaps they lower their voices conspiratorially at the same time, so as not to be overheard, or giggle uproariously together when someone tells a story.

In NLP this is known as *rapport*, which has been defined as the establishment of trust, harmony and co-operation in a relationship. The state or process of being in rapport with someone is often described as being 'in tune' or 'on the same wavelength' as them.

Rapport is usually achieved without us consciously having to try or even think about it. It's a natural phenomenon. When we're getting along with people we're in rapport most of the time. It's a fundamental part of effective communication and a vital component to building and maintaining successful relationships with others.

Unless you plan to live like Robinson Crusoe on an island, with no Man Friday, you'll need to get along with people, and this means having good rapport skills. If you want to be successful and popular you'll need to be able to connect and engage with others.

When we meet people for the first time and discover we share common interests it makes it easier for us to break the ice and establish rapport. We often know when we're in or out of rapport with another person by the way we feel inside. When we're in rapport it can feel like you're in 'flow' with the other person and when we're out of rapport it can feel awkward.

Because rapport is natural some people think it can't be learnt, but there are numerous ways that skills can be enhanced, and we'll be covering the most important ones in this chapter. In simple terms this involves behaving more like the other person, using your sensory acuity skills to pay attention to what they're doing and saying.

Matching and mirroring

Only a small part of human communication is achieved through what we actually say. The rest is non-verbal: gestures, facial expressions, posture, eye movements, nods, breathing, and voice qualities such as tone, pitch and rhythm.

This means that one of the key ways we establish and build rapport is by reading these non-verbal communications and mirroring and matching them. In fact, body mirroring and matching to create rapport are among the earliest and best known NLP techniques.

It's important to take care when copying someone's physiology. If you do it overtly it can look as if you're making fun of them and break rapport. There's a fine line between matching and mimicking. If the other person does something and you follow straight afterwards they'll probably notice. You might get away with it once, but if you do it repeatedly they're sure to pick it up. If you wait 20–30 seconds it's likely to go unobserved.

Here are some things you can match:

* Whole body matching, where you adjust your stance or your whole seated body to match another person's. Note the angle of their spine.
* Upper or lower body matching, where you match either your upper or lower body to theirs.
* The way they move, slow and smooth or energetic and jerky. Some people move a lot, some move a little. Some move mainly on one side of the body or just one hand or foot. Others move both sides together.
* Head tilt or shoulder matching, to the left or right, forwards or backwards.
* Matching gestures, some people make large gestures, others small.
* Matching facial expressions, eye direction or even their blink rate.
* Breathing, patterns and rhythms.

Matching in practice

The next stage in learning about matching is to have a go yourself. It's a great opportunity to practise calibrating too. You can either take a risk and try matching in everyday situations or you may prefer to ask a friend if they'd be happy to help you in the early stages. If you choose the latter option don't tell them what you're doing. Just get them to discuss something they feel passionate about. As you listen to them, and acknowledge what they have to say, match their behaviour leaving a gap of around 20 seconds after they've done something before copying it. At this stage concentrate on the most obvious things: overall posture, hand gestures, foot movements, etc.

Initially it can feel strange matching others. But you quickly get used to it, and skilled at continuing to chat in a natural way as you do so. The biggest challenge is when the other person's non-verbal behaviour is very different from yours. If they make big gestures and you don't gesture much you may feel as if you're going outside your comfort zone. But stick with it, and you'll start to feel more comfortable in doing things you wouldn't normally do.

Voice

You can also match people in terms of their voice. This is particularly valuable when you're speaking to someone on the phone, where it's obviously impossible to match physical movement, but is equally valuable in face-to-face encounters.

Is their speech steady, all at the same pace, or are bits of it fast and others slow. Do they pause much? Are their sentences short? To the point. Just like this. Or do they wander about a bit, with lots of diversions, things said to one side, or expanding on areas of interest before finally, eventually, ultimately coming to an end.

The next time you answer the phone, listen carefully to what the other person sounds like before saying anything yourself. If they speak fast, you speak fast. If they're quiet, you're quiet. Copy them, but once again short of mimicry. If someone has an unusual vocal style or strong accent, they could think you're making fun of them.

Pacing and leading

Having matched someone, and gained rapport, you can begin to influence them, taking them in another direction. In NLP this is known as Pacing and Leading. If you enter the other person's world, and do what they're doing for a while, then subtly change your behaviour, they will often follow. You might, for instance, match someone's breathing rate (pace) for a few minutes and then change yours (lead), either to calm someone down or increase their energy or feeling of excitement. The next time you walk alongside someone match their pace and length of stride for a while. Then make a subtle change perhaps by slowing down and notice how they change their speed to match yours.

What's important is that you don't try to lead too soon, or the person may not follow. The principle can best be described as pace, pace, pace and then lead. The longer you pace, the more likely you are to succeed.

the
Meta Model

The Meta Model is a series of 'challenges' that can be used to 'recover' information that has been 'lost' in the process of describing experience. At first you may find it technical and complicated, but it's worth persevering because it's extremely powerful.

There are 12 'Meta Model' sets of questions in three categories: Deletion (information from the external world deleted to avoid overwhelm); Distortion (simplifying an experience); Generalization (using previous experiences to categorize information).

Using the Meta Model challenges can pay dividends in a range of situations, from asking precision questions in a business setting to solving psychological problems in a therapeutic context.

In fact, the Meta Model was the subject of the first NLP book, *The Structure of Magic*, which arose from the first modelling carried out by NLP's founders. They noticed that when the therapists they were observing asked certain kinds of questions, people became clearer about their issues and their problems disappeared.

The first NLP model was the Meta Model. It was developed when Richard Bandler and John Grinder modelled the language patterns used by successful therapists Virginia Satir and Fritz Perls. What they observed was that certain types of question had therapeutic benefit, in other words, people got better. By analysing the structure of these interventions Bandler and Grinder identified six patterns that they were able to use to replicate the results achieved by Satir and Perls. In addition, they tested many other syntactic distinctions from Chomsky's transformational grammar, in which Grinder was an expert, in the context of 'change work' and six were found to be effective. ('Change work' is where you are helping someone change. This is typically therapy or coaching, but could also extend to counselling and training.)

What these challenges do is help people recover lost information, reconnect to their internal experience, and so reconfigure their cognitive maps. The problem is not that the world is impoverished. It's the representations that people make of it, and then mistake for reality, that are lacking. Once their internal model is enriched they're able to function more effectively in the world.

Deep and surface structure

The Meta Model, like the linguistic model from which it drew its inspiration, makes a distinction between deep structure and surface structure. It's a tool for understanding how thoughts are translated into words. Transformational grammar suggests that each utterance or sentence can be analysed at two levels – surface and deep structure.

The surface structure represents the actual order of the words in a sentence. The following two sentences, for instance, have the same surface structure even though the words are slightly different: 'The walls were painted by a new decorator' and 'The walls were painted by a new technique'. The deep structure of the two sentences is different because they don't have the same meaning. Now take these two sentences: 'A manager wrote the project report' and 'The project report was written by a manager'.

In this case the deep structure is the same even though the order of the words is different. The deep structure represents the basic grammatical relationships from which a sentence is derived.

In NLP this deep structure of what we seek to communicate is our complete internal representation, the mental images, sounds and feelings stored at the neurological, unconscious level of the mind. What we actually say or think is the surface structure. This is a greatly reduced version of our actual experience because in the course of moving from the deep structure to the surface structure three processes take place: distortion, deletion and generalization.

Elements of the Meta Model

Deletion

It would be impossible for us to pay attention to every stimulus around us. Our brain would be completely overloaded. In fact, George Miller and others have found that on average we can hold only seven (plus or minus two) items in consciousness at one time, though our unconscious mind has a greater capacity than that. As a result, at any particular moment we are tuning in to certain aspects of our experience and filtering out others. This reduces it to a level we can handle.

Distortion

The process of simplifying an experience inevitably leads to distortion. Sometimes we don't have all the information, and jump to conclusions that are unwarranted. But that doesn't mean it's a bad thing. Distortion is also a creative process, allowing us to imagine or fantasize about things that haven't yet happened, or come up with discoveries and inventions.

Generalization

Our ability to generalize is also essential when it comes to coping in the world. Using previous experiences that are similar as a starting point allows us to learn quickly. Imagine if every time you went to open a door you had to figure out how to do it.

Sometimes, though, our minds make generalizations that aren't an accurate representation of reality. One element of an experience comes to represent an entire category. We have a bad experience when having our car serviced and come to the conclusion that all mechanics are rude.

Challenging Meta Model 'violations'

Deletion, distortion and generalization are essential processes in the transformation of deep structure experience to a surface structure communication. Most of the time they work effectively in reducing the volume of information to manageable proportions while still representing the external world in a useful way. But not always. Sometimes problems occur. And the purpose of the Meta Model is to identify deletions, distortions and generalizations that are problematic by analysing the surface structure statements.

For each of the 12 distinctions that are defined by the Meta Model there are a series of challenges that aim to recover some of the information lost in the transformation from deep to surface structure. By asking certain kinds of questions when faced with a particular type of violation, the person is required to access the information that has been lost.

Challenging deletion

There are four principle ways in which information is deleted in the progression from deep structure to surface structure and as you might imagine the focus of any intervention is to recover what's been left out.

Simple deletion

Violation: An important element, such as an object, person or event, has been left out of a statement.

Objective: To recover the element that's been omitted.

Example: 'I'm sad.'

Response: 'Sad about what?'

Comparative deletion

Violation:	A comparison is implied in the statement but it doesn't say what it's being compared to.
Objective:	To establish what the comparison is being made against.
Example:	'It's better to go along with things.'
Response:	'Better than what?'

Lack of referential index

Violation:	The noun, object, person or event isn't specified.
Objective:	To clarify what is being referred to in the statement by recovering the noun.
Example:	'They are kind to me.'
Response:	'Who, specifically, is kind to you?'

Unspecified verbs

Violation:	A verb is not clearly defined.
Objective:	To define more precisely what's being done.
Example:	'I explain things badly.'
Response:	'How, specifically, do you explain things badly?'

Challenging distortion

We have a tendency to believe that our perspective on the world is accurate and the only one that's right, when in reality it's not only partial but distorted in a variety of ways.

Cause and effect

Violation:	A causal relationship is implied by the statement.
Objective:	To clarify the causal relationship.
Example:	'He really drives me crazy!'
Response:	'How, specifically, does he drive you crazy?'

Mind reading

Violation:	Where someone claims to know what someone else is thinking.
Objective:	To identify the thinking underlying that assumption.

Example:	'She thinks I'm lazy.'
Response:	'How do you know she thinks that?'

Complex equivalence

Violation:	Two different experiences are said to be the same thing.
Objective:	To establish the validity of the relationship.
Example:	'I failed my exam – I'm a complete loser.'
Response:	'How does failing your exam make you a loser?'

Lost performatives

Violation:	A statement expresses an opinion dressed up as fact.
Objective:	Identify the criteria used to make the judgement.
Example:	'It's not right for women to work when they have children.'
Response:	'Not right according to whom?'/'Who says?'

Nominalizations

Violation:	A verb has been made into a noun.
Objective:	To turn the statement into a process statement.
Example:	'There's too much confusion.'
Response:	'What's confusing you?'

Challenging generalization

Everybody generalizes all the time – like we just did! Management never tells the truth; I always help other people; time is a great healer. Such statements are rarely true, and when examined carefully sometimes prove to have no basis in fact, yet important decisions and actions are based upon them. Examining them can determine when they can be relied upon and when more subtle distinctions about the nature of the world are required.

Universal quantifiers

Violation:	A broad generalization using words such as 'all', 'every', 'never', 'everybody', 'always'.
Objective:	To check for counter-examples.

| Example: | 'He's never on time.' |
| Response: | 'Never?'/'Not even once?' |

Modal operators of necessity and possibility

Violation:	Statements that limit behaviour, using words such as 'can', 'can't', 'should', 'must', 'ought', 'necessary'.
Objective:	To identify the thinking behind the statement.
Example:	'I must go to the gym three times a week.' (necessity)
Response:	'What would happen if you didn't go?'

| Example: | 'I can't delegate.' (possibility) |
| Response: | 'What stops you?'/'What would happen if you did?' |

Presuppositions

Violation:	Something is implicitly required to make sense of the statement.
Objective:	To clarify the processes presupposed in the statement.
Example:	'If they cared for me they'd behave differently.'
Response:	'How do you know they don't care for you?'

Putting it all together

When you first start working with the Meta Model it can be a challenge tracking all 12 possible violations, and you may find it easier to focus on just one or two at a time. When you've got the hang of them you can do another couple. A good way to practise is by listening to the radio, where there's no visual element to distract you, and you can have this book to hand if you find it helpful.

10

key NLP techniques

Richard Bandler, John Grinder and many other NLP-ers who followed in their footsteps have created scores of amazing, powerful techniques that can be used to aid personal and professional development – and can be used to greatly enhance the quality of people's lives.

Using the Fast Phobia Cure, it's possible to cure some phobias – which may have been in place for many years – in less than 10 minutes. The New Behaviour Generator enables you, as the name suggests, to develop and strengthen new behaviours. And with Change Personal History, the experience of difficult, emotional or traumatic memories from childhood can be changed.

The benefits of NLP can be applied in almost any area of life including: personal development, presenting, sports, health, fitness, relationships, therapy, business, selling, negotiation, coaching, leadership, training, education and even spirituality. The only limit is your imagination, and NLP can help with that too!

Working with 'parts'

In the NLP model we all consist of a multitude of sub-personalities or parts that were created to carry out a particular purpose. That is, they have a positive intention. Sometimes, however, parts get disconnected from the context in which they were intended to operate, or even 'forget' what they were trying to do in the first place. Others continue to run even when the reason for their existence has long since passed, becoming a nuisance in the process.

Many people, for example, start to smoke around the age of 14, to feel more grown up and to impress their friends. Yet many years later the part responsible is still active, which is one of the reasons why it can be difficult to give up smoking.

A part is not just a temporary emotional state or habitual thought patterns. It's a discreet and autonomous mental system that has an idiosyncratic range of emotion, style of expression and set of abilities, intentions and functions.

Richard Schwartz

You may find it useful to think of a part as a computer program that was installed at a particular time for a good reason but then continues to run when it's no longer needed. And sometimes programs, or parts, conflict. Part of you may want to work, another part play. Happily, using NLP, such programs can be updated or uninstalled if necessary or where parts are in conflict they can be organized in such a way that they operate in harmony rather than antagonism.

It's also good to remember that 'parts' is just a useful way of thinking about how we organize our internal experience. We don't actually have parts inside us.

Six-step reframing

One of NLP's best-known techniques, and one of the first patterns to be developed by John Grinder in 1976, is called 'six-step reframing'. It's used when someone is unhappy with an aspect of their behaviour which they'd like to change. This could be a habit such as biting their nails; some kind of impulse, such as butting in when someone else is talking during a meeting; or even a physical symptom, such as a chronic headache.

As you might imagine from the name, the pattern consists of six steps, and these need to be carried out strictly in sequence. The 'reframing' element involves separating the problematic behaviour from its positive intention, so that actions which on the surface appear to be negative are understood to have been trying to achieve something for the person. It's a context reframe, because although the behaviour would be appropriate in other situations, it's not producing the desired outcome here. Different ways of satisfying the positive intention are then generated, which don't have the undesirable effects of the original behaviour.

Six-step reframing is an extremely powerful and effective pattern, and one which needs to be used carefully. You can do it with yourself or with other people. The version here is for personal use.

Steps

1 Allow yourself to relax fully and turn your attention inwards, thinking only about the behaviour you want to change.

2 Establish communication with the 'part' that's responsible for the behaviour by asking, in your mind, 'Please give me a signal if you are willing to communicate with me'. Be aware of anything that changes, such as internal sounds, images or feelings. If you get what may be a signal, but it's weak, invite the part to 'Please make the signal stronger if the answer is yes.' Thank the part for even the smallest response. If you have ignored a part for some time it may need some coaxing. (If you receive no signal after a number of times of asking, you may have to consider another approach to the problem.)

3 When you have a clear, unambiguous signal, the next step is to discover the positive intention behind the problematic behaviour. Ask 'What is it you are trying to do for me

or communicate to me that's positive by means of this behaviour?' You may hear a voice in your head or simply 'know' the answer. Don't try to figure out consciously what it might be, just allow it to emerge. If the answer seems to be negatively stated, first thank the part and then simply ask again, 'What is your positive purpose?'

4 Once you know what that purpose is, say 'Please go now to your creative part and ask it to come up with three new ways to satisfy the positive intention'. It may produce a symbol, sound or some other response that doesn't make much sense to your conscious mind. Just go with what ever comes up. Some people don't think of themselves as being creative and are surprised when they discover this part. Putting a limit of three gives you a real choice and also prevents your creative part from continuing to supply you with an endless number of useful suggestions. It really is that creative!

5 Once you have those three ways, ask the part responsible for the problematic behaviour to confirm that it accepts the alternative choice(s) by using the same signal as before. Sometimes a particular choice is not acceptable, and you need to go back and generate more choices.

6 Finally, carry out an ecology check by asking whether any other parts object to these new choices being implemented. If you do find there are ecological concerns, you need to go back to Step 2 and repeat the process, making contact with that part and discovering its positive intention, etc.

Other techniques

NLP is famous for its amazingly fast, effective and safe techniques for curing phobias, improving confidence, and dealing with trauma and a host of other issues. Many of these patterns originated as simpler and quicker ways of carrying out therapy, and arose out of modelling. To demonstrate the diversity and flexibility of NLP in action we're discussing three different types of techniques in this chapter.

New Behaviour Generator

Are there situations where you would like to behave differently? Perhaps there's something you'd like to do but don't know how. Maybe you want to be more confident in a social setting. Or motivated to go to the gym. If so, the New Behaviour Generator holds the key to success. As the name indicates, it's a process that allows you to generate new behaviours – or, in NLP-speak, install a new strategy, program or part (depending on how you prefer to think of it) with a particular function.

When you use it you systematically create an internal sensory-specific representation of the behaviour you want. The reason it works so well is that our unconscious minds can't tell the difference between what happens and what we imagine because they share the same neurology. In practice it's a bit like a dress rehearsal. Using an 'as if' frame you create a new mental map of the behaviour you want. You try the new 'you' on for size and check kinaesthetically to find out if anything's missing or needs to be added. If there is, you make a few adjustments. It really is that simple. Try it out for yourself using the process outlined below.

Steps
1 Identify a behaviour you would like to have, and be clear what the outcome of having it would be for you.
2 See yourself, either in your mind's eye or as if you are standing in front of yourself, in the future carrying out the desired behaviour as you would like to.
3 Remaining dissociated – like a movie director – make whatever changes seem necessary to the action and soundtrack, so that the 'other' you performs the new behaviour easily and effortlessly. Continue making adjustments to your imagined scenario until you are totally happy. Be aware as you do so of the reactions of other people to the changes you've made.
4 In your imagination, step into that other you and, in an associated state, experience doing the new behaviour – seeing, hearing and feeling what it's like.

5 Carry out an ecology check to make sure that the new behaviour fits with your values and your sense of self.

6 If anything's not as it should be, go back to being the movie director and make whatever changes are necessary before stepping back into yourself.

7 Think of at least one future occasion when you will want to use the new behaviour, and imagine yourself performing in that situation.

If you use this technique regularly you'll find it becomes almost second nature – you could find yourself using it on a daily basis. One way of getting it 'into the muscle' is to carry out a personal review at the end of each day. Ask yourself what went well and what didn't go as well as you would have liked. For the things that could have been better use the New Behaviour Generator. It's a powerful way of propelling yourself forward to where you want to be.

Fast Phobia Cure

based on the work of Richard Bandler

Spiders, snakes, heights, confined spaces, flying, thunderstorms or even public speaking – everyone knows someone who has a phobia. Maybe you're a sufferer yourself. *The Collins English Dictionary* defines a phobia as an 'abnormal, intense and irrational fear of a given situation, organism or object'. Typical symptoms include dizziness, heart palpitations and a sense of terror. When the stimulus appears – sometimes it only needs to be thought of – the person responds automatically with a strong physical reaction. Some phobias can be hard to live with, and many limit people in what they can do.

There are various schools of opinion on how phobias are formed but NLP has no real interest in causes. The main focus of NLP therapy is on how problems are handled in the present. The event itself has long since passed into the mists of time, so it must be the way the person is representing it internally that's causing the difficulty. When they're exposed to whatever makes them phobic they associate back to a picture they have of the memory, and experience all of the emotion again.

When you're dissociated, though, and looking at events as an observer, you can't have the bad feelings. And that's the principle at the heart of the Fast Phobia Cure, which uses double-dissociation to distance people from the emotions they felt originally. Although it's called a 'phobia cure', the pattern can also be used with any trauma or fear where the response to a stimulus is instantaneous. But it's not suitable for situations where anxiety or dread builds up over a period of time.

Steps

This is a powerful technique, and it's important to follow all of the steps in the order shown.

1 Imagine you're in a cinema. Choose a seat somewhere towards the back while you wait for the film to start. See yourself up on the screen in a still black and white picture just before the original phobic incident took place, or if you can't remember, one of the most intense episodes you ever had ...

2 Now float back inside the projection room. (If you are phobic about heights, just walk there.) You are now in a safe, secure observer position and able to see yourself sitting in your seat in the cinema looking relaxed.

3 Remaining in the projection booth, continue to watch yourself as you allow a black and white film of the phobic incident to run on the screen. When it reaches the end, stop the film and turn it into a still picture.

4 Now leave the projection room and step into the still picture on the screen. Change the picture to colour and then run the film backwards as fast as possible – 1 to 2 seconds – experiencing it from inside. Repeat this process several times.

5 Try to access the phobic state by thinking about the stimulus. You should now have no trouble thinking about it. If some discomfort remains, do the process once again.

11

modelling

'Modelling' is at the heart of NLP: the idea is that if you study someone who is excellent at something, and understand how they do it, you too can be excellent at it.

Bandler and Grinder showed this to be true when NLP first began in the 1970s by modelling three of the foremost therapists of the time. They discovered that by copying their techniques and language patterns, they were able to bring about change in people they worked with.

At its simplest, modelling involves watching another person. This can be effective for simple tasks. At a more sophisticated level, it involves eliciting the person's beliefs, values and 'thinking filters'.

Businesses and consulting companies, for instance, often use modelling to benchmark top performers – such as the best sales people – so as to be able to share their skills with everyone else in the team.

What would it be like if you could play the guitar like Eric Clapton or golf like Tiger Woods? Imagine being able to have any skill you want – and learning it quickly and easily, without having to slog away for years or waste time by trial and error. And what would it be worth if you could discover how the top performers in your company achieve their success, then replicate it? How would it be if your best salesperson, manager, negotiator, etc. could act as a template for the rest of the team, reproducing 'best practice' throughout the organization?

If that sounds like a pipe dream to you, think again. Right from the very beginning, with the studies Richard Bandler and John Grinder carried out on Perls, Satir, Erickson and others, the principle purpose of NLP has been the modelling of human excellence. And it has been demonstrated time and again that once you understand the thinking patterns and behaviours used by the most brilliant and talented in any field, you can learn to do what they can do.

Modelling has given birth to many fascinating and powerful techniques and processes, and a significant proportion of the major models, including the Meta Model and the Milton Model. These are often emphasized in books and on courses, with the result that some people mistakenly think of them as being NLP, when in fact, as John Grinder and Carmen Bostic St Clair argue passionately in *Whispering in the Wind*, modelling itself remains at the heart of NLP.

Understanding modelling

You may recall that one of the presuppositions we discussed way back in Chapter 2 is that, 'If one person can do something, anyone can learn to do it'. And although there are obviously exceptions – you may not have the build for a world champion weight lifter – it's essentially true. You may also recall another presupposition: 'Experience has a structure'. Put both presuppositions together and you have the rationale for modelling: once the structure that makes up the internal experience of an expert has been captured and encoded, it can be transferred to others, allowing them to achieve the same results. To be able to do this we have to break down what the person does into small enough chunks so we understand the deeper structure underlying their behaviour clearly enough to create a model that can then be explained to others.

Because modelling provides a short-cut to excellence there are many ways it can be applied. It's not about looking for someone who's superhuman, but it is about finding people who are skilled in a particular area – an athlete is not necessarily going to shine at mathematics or selling. There are many examples where modelling excellence has been applied in therapeutic work, sport, selling, negotiation, relationships, leadership, education, families and organizational development.

Natural modelling

People are natural modellers. From the moment we were born we started copying others, developing a multitude of skills and capabilities along the way. Somehow we internalize the rules of grammar and syntax simply by listening to our parents and siblings talk. In the playground and at home we watched others and imitated their behaviours. As adults wanting to learn a new skill such as playing a musical instrument, we look carefully at other people and do the same. NLP modelling is more purposeful and structured than natural modelling, which can be haphazard, and as a result produces accurate and reliable results.

Simple and complex modelling

The purpose of NLP modelling is, then, to be able to do something as well as an expert and to be able to teach others to do it as well.

The process by which the modelling is carried out will depend to a large degree upon what is being modelled. If it's something simple, with a largely behavioural element, it may be possible to model it in just a short while, simply by watching and matching. You may never have thrown a ball up against a wall, let it bounce and then caught it. But if you watched someone do it for a while and then had a go yourself, it wouldn't take long before you got the hang of it. It's the same with simple cognitive tasks: most people find it easy to assimilate a new way of remembering names, for instance, in just a few minutes.

However, more complex behavioural and cognitive tasks, which have a greater number of steps or perhaps a linguistic component, require a different approach.

If you wanted to learn how to play badminton, for instance, most of the basic skills could be absorbed by an alert observer in less than an hour, without the need for explanation. By carefully noting the position of the shuttlecock, the angle of the racquet and the way it's held, the stance and movement of the players, etc., it would normally be possible to play a game with an acceptable degree of competence. But to play with any degree of skill would depend upon having a more sophisticated internal representation of the game.

Implicit and explicit modelling

If you ever undertake NLP Practitioner training, you may find yourself following a fellow student around for 20 minutes, trying to walk and move like them. It's a simple but effective way of learning the principles and methodology of modelling. This is called implicit modelling, which involves acting like your model and building intuitions about what's going on for them. It's similar to the apprentice/master relationship in martial arts where the simple act of being with the master allows the apprentice to absorb what the master does.

But why not simply ask the person what they're doing and why? That may sometimes be useful, but one of the hurdles we have to overcome when modelling is that many people don't know what makes them successful. Or they may think they know, but are wrong. Once we become accomplished at doing something, we no longer have to pay attention to how we do it. There are four stages in acquiring a skill:

* Unconscious incompetence, when we're not even aware of what it is possible for us to do.
* Conscious incompetence, when we know we don't know how to do something.
* Conscious competence, when we're aware we're doing something correctly.
* Unconscious competence, when the skill becomes automatic and we do it without thinking about it.

To create a transferable model we have to uncover a person's unconscious competence (implicit phase), and become consciously competent and attain the result ourselves (explicit phase).

Implicit modelling, then, is an intuitive process of understanding the other person's subjective experience by putting ourselves in their shoes. In contrast, explicit modelling is a dissociated and deductive process of working out the specific structure of the role model's subjective experience.

12

the Milton Model

Remember the Meta Model we discussed in Chapter 9 and the different questions you could ask to retrieve 'missing' information? Well the Milton model is the exact opposite – with a few other categories thrown in for good measure.

Named after Milton Erickson, who was in his day the world's foremost hypnotherapist, the Milton Model consists of language that is deliberately, 'artfully' vague. The ambiguity of the language helps induce trance, making people more open to suggestion and persuasion.

These language patterns are useful when you're doing change work with people. You can speak directly with their unconscious mind, without them realizing consciously what you are doing.

Erickson would often bring about therapeutic change simply by telling people stories, based around the different categories of the Milton Model.

You are curious. And that means you can learn faster. As you become aware of your feelings you will relax. Because NLP is fascinating, isn't it? People always grasp things easily when they're comfortable. Could you reflect deeply on a memory? And as your mind wanders, all the way down, you know it's right now. Will you let go immediately, or in a moment? Fortunately it's no problem. They say, 'You can have whatever you want'. Understanding is valuable. Don't imagine it's not true. Reflecting on your experiences will make you realize what's important.

What was your reaction to that opening paragraph? Did it make perfect sense to you, or did it seem a bit strange? Are you perhaps tempted to call in the Meta Model police and arrest it for multiple violations?

The introduction was, in fact, carefully and methodically crafted using the Milton Model, a set of linguistic patterns developed by Richard Bandler and John Grinder in 1975 from their modelling of Milton H. Erickson, one of the world's leading hypnotherapists, and the founder of the American Society for Clinical Hypnosis.

Bandler and Grinder studied Erickson's therapeutic approach in great detail over a period of some months, using implicit modelling as described in Chapter 11. What they were fascinated to discover was that the language he used when treating clients was very different from that used by Perls and Satir, which had formed the basis of the Meta Model. In fact, it was almost as if Erickson were wilfully violating as many of the Meta Model patterns as possible.

Whereas Perls and Satir asked questions to help recover deleted information and reveal distortions and generalizations, Erickson would often tell stories that were vague and ambiguous. The Meta Model worked by helping the client develop internal maps that were more accurate and therefore more useful in achieving their desired outcomes. The Milton Model was equally effective but what was the secret of its success?

Being artfully vague

In their book *The Patterns of the Hypnotic Techniques of Milton H. Erickson MD*, Bandler and Grinder describe the language patterns used by Erickson as 'artfully vague'. He deliberately produced sentences that were open to a range of interpretations, in direct contrast to the specificity of the Meta Model. In essence, what he was doing was intentionally creating distortions, deletions and generalizations.

NLP and hypnosis

Milton Model language is valuable when doing any kind of change work with other people.

Asking people questions, such as those in the Meta Model, engages people in reality processing. In NLP this is called 'uptime', where conscious thinking predominates. Getting people to focus on their experience, their internal representation, takes them into trance, or 'downtime' as it's sometimes referred to in NLP.

Is NLP, then, simply hypnosis by another name? Certainly, during many patterns and processes people clearly go into trance, and that can facilitate change. But as we've seen, there's a lot more to NLP than the Milton Model and trancework.

Inverse Meta Model categories

Let's start by looking at the aspects of the Milton Model that are the inverse of the Meta Model. As you read them reflect on how you will apply each one sooner or later.

Simple deletions

Deliberately leaving information out of a communication results in the listener asking questions and seeking answers. Consider: 'It can now be told'. What can be told to whom by whom in what way, and why only now? We don't know, it's not clear.

Example:

'This makes sense.'

Comparative deletion

If, when making a comparison, you don't indicate what's being evaluated against what, you create confusion and stimulate a transderivational search (a search of your memories and experiences) for the missing information. In the example below we don't know what the starting point is: 'More than what?' and 'Better than what?'

Example:

'They want more.'

Lack of referential index

When it's not clear who is doing something, people have to draw upon their own experiences to understand a statement. In the example, who precisely knows?

Example:

'They know all the answers.'

Unspecified verb

When verbs aren't specified, the listener is required to fill in the details themself to make sense of the communication. Verbs that can work in this way include 'experience', 'feel', 'understand', 'sense' and 'learn'.

Example:

'You can understand how you will feel better.'

Cause and effect – causal linkage

People naturally think in causal terms, with one thing following on as a consequence from another. 'The deadline's approaching and I need to work hard', or 'The telephone call made me late for the meeting'. Presenting ideas in the form of two statements that are linked can be extremely persuasive, moving the person in the direction of the desired behaviour. If the first is verifiable in experience the unconscious mind will often accept the linkage as true, even when there's no basis in fact. As the NLP trainer Tad James is fond of saying in his workshops, 'It doesn't have to be true, it just has to be plausible.'

Conjunction

This is the simplest and weakest kind of linkage, where any two phrases are connected using words such as: 'and', 'but', 'for', 'yet' and 'so'.

Example:

'You can notice your breathing and begin to relax.'

Implied causative

A stronger linkage is created by an implied causative, which uses 'If... then...', 'during', 'while', 'soon' or 'as you/so you...' to connect the statements.

Example:

'If you consider these patterns then you can learn them easily.'

Cause—effect

This is the strongest form of linkage, with the causality made explicit, using words such as 'makes', 'forces', and 'that means'.

Example:

'The sound of my voice will make you feel comfortable.'

Because the causal link is more evident when using implied causative and cause—effect patterns, it can be useful to use negative phrasing, because it's harder for the person to keep track of what's being connected.

Example:

'You won't be able to resist getting more curious as you hear what's coming next.'

Mind reading

Claiming to know what the other person is thinking can make suggestions more credible and strengthen rapport. Care needs to be taken to keep comments general to avoid a clash with their actual experience.

Example:

'I know you are curious about what's going to happen.'

Complex equivalence

Two statements can be equated as having the same meaning by the way they're linked together. The easiest way is by using 'that means'.

Example:

'You're learning NLP, that means you're interested in people.'

Lost performative

Being able to present a judgement or evaluation as fact, without saying whose judgement or evaluation it is, can be valuable in by-passing resistance. One of the simplest ways is to use the word 'It's'.

Example:

'It's useful to understand the way lost performatives work.'

Nominalization

As we discussed in Chapter 9, nominalizations are abstract nouns that have been created out of process words, such as 'happiness' and 'curiosity', which derive from being happy and curious. These are great words to use because they allow people to attach their own meaning to them.

Example:

'You can take satisfaction in your knowledge.'

Universal quantifiers

Presenting communications as if they were universal generalizations can make them more credible, especially to the unconscious mind, which may not examine them closely. Key words to use include 'all', 'every', 'nobody', 'always', 'everyone' and 'never'.

Example:

'People always learn more easily when they relax.'

Modal operators

The two modal operators of necessity and possibility can be used to suggest rules and orient experience in a particular direction.

The modal operators of necessity – should/shouldn't, must/mustn't, have to/don't have to – can be used to limit choice.

Example:

'And you don't even have to try, it can all happen naturally by itself.'

Use can/can't, will/won't, able/unable for the modal operators of possibility.

Example:

'You are able to come up with many creative ideas.'

Presuppositions

It's possible to elicit agreement indirectly by including assumptions or presuppositions in your statement or question. Because they're taken for granted, but not made explicit, they often don't get noticed by the conscious mind. There are various types of presuppositions, as follows:

Examples:

'You can deepen your understanding while you read this book.'

'We'll come to the third example in a minute...'

Double binds

Double binds utilize presuppositions to present an illusory choice – whichever option is taken leads to the desired outcome.

Example:

'Shall we discuss things here or in your office.'

Additional Milton Model patterns

Awareness (factive) predicates

Using words such as know, realize, notice and aware presupposes that what's being said is true.

Adverbs and adjectives

Slipping in an adverb here and there is a simple but powerful way of presupposing that something's happening by focusing on the nature of the experience. Useful adverbs include deeply, surprisingly, happily, luckily, readily and easily.

Commentary adjectives and adverbs

Sentences can be structured so that everything after the first word is supposed. Useful words are happily, fortunately, usefully.

Quotes

When you want to communicate something directly, but feel you can't for whatever reason, one option is to use quotes. As we tell a story or recount a conversation we often quote verbatim what was said, such as: 'Then he said to me, "You need to *make that change now*"'. While listeners will recognize the statement as being for the person in the story, their unconscious mind will register it as a command directed at them, especially when special emphasis is given to the words.

Embedded commands

An embedded command is a message or instruction that's hidden or embedded in a sentence. It works subliminally, because although the conscious mind won't recognize it, the unconscious mind will. Using commands in this way makes it possible to give suggestions indirectly. The effect is heightened if you use analogue marking – lowering the voice tone and increasing the volume slightly – when saying the words that make up the command. You don't have to be obvious when doing so, the unconscious mind is remarkably sensitive to subtlety.

Embedded questions

Words such as 'wonder', 'curious', 'know' and 'understand' have a particular value because they make it possible to ask questions to which no response is expected. A message can therefore be communicated in an indirect manner.

Negative commands

In Chapter 4 we discussed the difficulty the mind has when processing negatively phrased statements such as 'Don't think of a guitar'. To be able to *not* think of it, you have to *think* of it. Phrasing a command negatively is particularly effective with people who mismatch.

Conversational postulate

Openly requesting information or action can sometimes generate resistance but that can be avoided by using the conversational postulate (e.g. 'Could you pass me the file?'). It sounds like a question but it's really a command!

Ambiguity

Ambiguity is when words or statements have a double meaning, and are open to interpretation. In NLP-speak, there's more than one possible deep structure for a particular surface structure. Ambiguity therefore stimulates a transderivational search to find the most appropriate meaning.

Pacing current experience

One of the most effective ways of establishing rapport with someone is to make statements that match their current experience. Doing so narrows the person's attention to what they're seeing, hearing and feeling, and encourages them to go inside. For that reason it's useful to incorporate visual, auditory and kinaesthetic statements that the person will recognize as true. You can then follow on with statements that lead them into trance. As a rule of thumb, give three pacing statements before trying to lead. As you become aware of your breathing, hear the sounds in the room, and focus on the words on this page, so you can relax.

Tag questions

You can distract the conscious mind, and so displace resistance, by adding a question at the end of a statement, don't you think? The communication then goes directly to the unconscious mind, which is what you want, isn't it? Useful questions to tag at the end include won't you?, didn't I?, and aren't you?

Selectional restriction violation

This complicated sounding technique involves attributing feelings to inanimate objects, concepts and animals, which they could not have. One of the most famous examples of this technique is documented and analysed in *Patterns of the Hypnotic Techniques of Milton H. Erickson MD*. During a session focused primarily on pain control, Erickson talked to Joe, a retired farmer, about growing tomato plants. He told him, for instance, that tomato plants can feel relaxed and comfortable. Generally when people hear this type of statement they make sense of it by assuming it refers to them in some way.

Metaphor

Although Milton Erickson was sometimes directive in his approach, most of the time he simply told his clients stories. As you might imagine, they were not just random stories. They were carefully chosen or created to fit the needs of each particular person. Over many years of practice and research Erickson refined his skills, and was able to facilitate spectacular changes with seemingly difficult cases. There are many fascinating books available that document his imaginative interventions.

Quite a lot of NLP thinking is based upon Erickson's work, and many of the presuppositions – that people have all the resources they need, that all behaviours have a positive intention, etc. – originated with him. The idea of using stories has also been adopted. This is known in NLP as metaphor, with the term covering a wide range of interventions, including analogies, jokes, parables, similes, fables and allegories as well as stories and metaphors.

As Carl Jung and others have shown, metaphor is the natural language of the unconscious mind, and when utilized effectively speaks directly to the deepest part of a person. It also communicates in a way that bypasses the conscious mind, making it more difficult to resist or sabotage the message.

NLP in action

By now you understand how powerful NLP can be, but it's only when you put it into practice on a daily basis that you fully appreciate what it can do for you. Here's a brief introduction to some of the most popular uses.

NLP and personal development

People come to NLP for many reasons, and one of the most common is personal development. It's not unusual for those attending NLP workshops to make significant changes in their life.

Sometimes this is as a result of the Well-Formed Outcome process. They ask themselves, perhaps for the first time in a long while, What do I want? They may well get more in touch with their values, starting to live in a way that's more aligned with them.

NLP provides a range of tools for expanding your self-awareness and your awareness of others. People learn to manage their emotions better, taking control of them rather than – as is sometimes the case – being victims of them.

But it's often the 'P' part of NLP that makes the most important difference. They change their 'programs', sometimes installing new ones, sometimes updating them to the latest version, and sometimes uninstalling programs that no longer work or serve them. As a result they develop more effective strategies and habits which make them happier and more effective.

NLP in sports and fitness

Sport is not just a physical battle – there's also a mental battle, and that's the one that can be really challenging. Physical fitness has to be matched by mental fitness.

This is, of course, where NLP techniques come into their own, and why they're so widely used by professional sports psychologists when they're working with their clients – and why they're equally effective for amateurs. Visualization techniques are commonly used to install new habits at the neurological level. This can involve recalling and re-accessing peak experiences in the past, stepping mentally into the body of a role model, or acting as a film director and creating a movie in which the person has all the resources they need.

NLP in business

Communication lies at the heart of every business. It's an essential ingredient for success that we cannot afford to ignore. Whatever your role you'll benefit from learning more about yourself and how to interact with others more effectively.

Rapport skills, for instance, help us to build good relationships with people we come into contact with on a day-to-day basis. In essence NLP helps people become more effective communicators.

People who work in any area of a business benefit from improved communication. Meetings are more effective, teams work together cohesively, the right people are recruited and more business is won through a highly skilled sales team.

NLP in health and well-being

One of presuppositions of NLP is that the mind and body are one system – the thoughts we have affect what goes on in our body and vice-versa. And this has been proved to be the case on countless occasions. You need only consider the placebo effect to know it to be true. A whole new discipline has, in fact, grown up that deals with this relationship: psycho-neuro-immunology. NLP can be a powerful tool in maintaining both your mental and physical health and well-being, with numerous tools and techniques to help you keep on track.

Whatever you want, whatever you need

While NLP is not 'snake oil'. capable of curing every malady, it is one of the most powerful tools available for personal and professional transformation. Taken daily, it is capable of giving you whatever you want and whatever you need.